Seen From The Gallery

Also by Maureen Sudlow

Fearless Fred and the Dragon
Fearless Fred and the Flood
Children's picture books in rhyme

Antipodes

Seen From The Gallery

Maureen Sudlow

Seen From The Gallery

A Wordly Press Publication
Ashhurst, New Zealand
Phone 64 6 326 8066

First published by Wordly Press in 2017

Copyright © Maureen Sudlow 2017

All rights reserved. No part of this publication may be reproduced, stored in a retrieval system, or transmitted in any form or by any means, electronic, mechanical, including photocopying, recording or otherwise without prior written permission from the author.

The author asserts her moral right to be identified as the author of this work.

'Seen from the gallery' was published in *Take Flight* August 2015;

'They also serve' was published in *When Anzac Day Comes Around, 100 years from Gallipoli Poetry Project* by Graeme Lindsay.

All photographs taken by the author

ISBN 978-0-9941478-0-6

A catalogue record for this book is available from the National Library of New Zealand.

Wordly Press
www.wordlypress.com

*Publishing a volume of verse is like dropping
a rose petal down the Grand Canyon and
waiting for the echo — Don Marquis*

Contents

Gone	1
Seen From The Gallery	2
Shadows	3
Autumn By the River	4
Hansen's Boatyard	5
Before	6
The Gulls	7
Feelings	8
Recycling	9
Northland By-Election	9
Impressions	10
Resurrection	11
Who	12
In the Path of the Cyclone	13
Interlude	14
Electronic Travels In Australia	15
Long Distance Loneliness	16
Silver-Eye	17
Salt	18
Falling	20
Tweeting	21
Birdlings Flat	22
Counting Down	23
Always This Moment	24

Retribution	26
Partridges and Other Things	27
After the Drought	28
Just a Muff	29
Who's Counting	30
They Also Serve	32
Chunuk Bair	33
Karanga	34
Omens	36
Last Leaves	37
Ripples	38
Progression	40
Haiku	41
Water and Wine	42
Walking	43
Austin Kleon	44
This Day	45
Missing	46
Journey	48
To the City	49
Love	50
Memories	51

GONE

boats don't call any more
where the old wharf sags
at the river's bend
and the rice grass
moves with the tide

and home — was just
over the next horizon

Seen From the Gallery

cloud builds behind the hills
as a couple kiss passionately
by the picnic tables…

after the downpour
no one left except two seagulls
squabbling over crumbs

Shadows

shadows across the Northern Wairoa
as evening comes
bringing a halt to our work
and bathing the hills in the glow
of last light

beyond the grass
a grey heron
resting

Autumn By the River

autumn by the river
cages of wild parsley seeds
near the old road piles
and Tokatoka hiding
in the distant haze

the world and I
preparing for winter

Hansen's Boatyard

at the edge of the river
the old boatyard's up for sale
sand dredge no longer fussing
with the swell of the tide
only the slap of water, on rotting piles
and rice grass bending in the wind

don't know how long
I'll be able to stay,
the boatman says
I guess when it's sold
I'll have to go…

some man from the city
thinks it's worth a lot of money
but this is the Kaipara

Before

soft touch of mist
on the mountains beyond the river
a caress before the cold grip of winter
covers the land

a lone boat
heads out on the tide

The Gulls

Impeccable in morning coats
and fine feathers
orange gaiters on display
there by the shore they stand
just waiting for tomorrow
and the next rising
of the tide.

FEELINGS

smell of sunshine
on wind-dried sheets
the road home

cut grass
behind the mower
autumn song

railway track
where distant hills fade
into the unknown

RECYCLING

the neighbour is burning off
my washing smells of smoke
and recycled life

NORTHLAND BY-ELECTION

skinny dead cat
on the road this morning
politician's promises

Impressions

a cooler breeze today
sends the leaves waltzing
clouds sailing
the dog finding a patch of sun
on the deck

she walks slowly
one foot in front of the other
nothing lies ahead
everything behind
empty

old friends are always best
a warmth like well-aged wine
where we can rest awhile
and forget our slow decline
into oblivion…

sombre sky gathering clouds
as a woman gathers her skirts
the birds are silent
in the afternoon heat
praying for rain

distracted by kereru
tumbling around the branches
of the liquidambar
my book put aside
as they pass

Resurrection

I close my eyes
and there's only bird-song
only warmth, and the rattle
of nikau fronds

the distant, unexpected
crow of a rooster
light and dark, patterned
against my eyelids
only this moment, ever

Who

who can capture
the magic of starlight
the deepness of shadows
and the sudden flight
of a bird
from the thicket

In the Path of the Cyclone

storm building
as a butterfly flits past
my study window

we pick the ripe peaches
before they are lost
and I wonder if
the cicada's staccato
love song will survive

down on the flat
the river is running high

INTERLUDE

a grey heron
gathering the evening light
before the fading summer-long song
of cicada
gives way
to a cricket's autumn chirrup
and the long night
of winter

ELECTRONIC TRAVELS IN AUSTRALIA

We talked on the computer today
and you carried me outside with your tablet
to show me your treasured frog-pond.

For a while I caught glimpses
of grass, sky and various body parts
before being focused
on the bulging eyes
of a small, green, and very surprised frog.

Long Distance Loneliness

hum of conversation
hiss of coffee machines
indecipherable announcements
under jet engine roar

crowded airport
but I am alone
small and unnoticed
after you leave

Silver-Eye

a soft sound
as small grey feathers
tumble
from darting flight
to darkness

I hold in my hands
the remnants
of a song

SALT

across the harbour
wind whips the sea
into foaming lace

on the dock
a crane turns slowly
and a yacht with three bare masts
motors towards the wharf

FALLING

red of sunlight through closed eyelids
muted rush and rumble of waves
tumbling to shore

wind salt-warm against my skin
rustling through the marram grass
grit-feel of sand
beneath my feet

Tweeting

The morning news drove me out of bed. Atrocities, political shenanigans and everything in between. I mean, who needs to hear this. Thank God there's still some good news left in the world.

birdsong
cannot be described
in words

Birdlings Flat

old macrocarpa lean to the wind
shade the huts, where paint peels
from sun-burned weatherboards
scattered among ice-plants
and vagrant plastic bags

rattle of pebbles
as a wave sucks out
down the shingle bank
where the best stones lie

we gather treasures
gifted here from Tangaroa
in the knife-edge cut of the wind
never turning our backs on the sea

Counting Down

the clock chimes
counting down the hours
since you left

and I feel you here
just behind me
untouchable

I turn, suddenly
you are gone

just a glimpse
of light, rippling
where once you stood

and the scent of violets

Always This Moment

a painted boat
moored on mudflats
waiting for the tide

distant truck
changing gear on the long hill
drowned by a blackbird
singing

rushing flight
of kereru
above the trees

two monarch butterflies
dancing in the sun
before the next
long winter comes

coolness of clouds
diluting sunlight
presence of love

I will always
be a part of
this moment
this sunlight
this birdsong

RETRIBUTION

a hawk circling
above dry grass
on the ground
nothing moves

Partridges and Other Things

Christmas is over
but there is still a partridge
in next door's pear tree.

A fan is trying
to blow summer heat
back out the window.
On the deck
the thermometer has broken.

I thought I heard footsteps.
It was only Bill
overtaking me
on his naked horse.[1]

Wood pigeons
falling through the loquat trees.
Collateral damage.

Behind the rice grass
the river is fizzing
with drops of morning sun.
Prisms dancing
to the music of summer.

---

1   Reference to Bill Manhire "Declining the Naked Horse"

AFTER THE DROUGHT

For weeks the sky has been a hot blue dome, the grass brown and brittle on the dusty earth. Even the birds were quiet. But today, at last, clouds cover the sky. Torrential rain overflows the gutters.

in the street
children with turned up faces
dancing

Just a Muff

Do you remember Mother,
this old muff, found in your drawers
as we took on the task of moving?
How it warmed your old hands
when the blood flowed slowly
through your veins?

And I remember my own muff,
a warm and furry cave
that hid my hands
from winter's biting chill.
An illusion of warmth
in an indifferent world.

Who's Counting

A wood pigeon sits on the rail
outside my window,
fat white waistcoat
and iridescent shoulders,
his mind on the nikau berries
just beyond the deck.
He's checking first
to see if we're inside
and safe.
No sense in taking risks.

The cabbage trees this year
have flowered abundantly.
Old men shake their heads,
'Going to be a long, hot summer.'
But the cabbage trees
aren't saying a word.
Only the wood pigeons are counting.

Christmas at the beach
and there's sand in the sandwiches
again.

They Also Serve

The Last Post
tears recalled the ones
who waited
alone.

Flag-draped coffins
wheeled from the gape
of a Hercules
all that was left.
The flag drops slowly.

Vietnam, I remember
just another separation
one of many.

And now
Anzac reminds me
that I miss
those people
that place
who we were.

Chunuk Bair

do they hear again the bugle sound
at Chunuk Bair, the dead,
as the flags are raised once more
above the bay

where the sea washes gentle
against the bloodied rocks
do they hear the cannon roar
as on that day

or do they hear only
the silence, and the soft hush
of the waves
along the shore

Karanga

In the early dawn they gather
rank on rank; the bugle sounds
the old men with their medals
the families gathered round

but just beyond the shadows
out where darkness dims
where memories are whispering
the others gather in

they stand by their old comrades
in proud review they come
and ever on the morning chill
they hear the muffled drum

they come in from the battlefields
the beaches and the skies
from every place and every land
to where the loved flag flies

Haere mai, Haere mai...

Omens

clouds gather above the hills
the day grows dark around me
the grey heron flies home to its mate
bent wings in graceful arcs
before the storm

Last Leaves

last leaves holding to the trees
like old friends sharing memories
waiting for God

and the sun fading into winter
above the hills

Ripples

and on this grey morning
we walked along the riverbank
counting seagulls
and watching mullet jump
above the ripples

my hand cold in yours
bare branches against
the sky

before you left

PROGRESSION

from the people
the land is plundered
and sold

where are the protesters
the young people
the kaitiaki

we sit like frogs
in a slowly heating pot
until we boil

Haiku

arrival
the deep green curve
of a breaking wave

bees drunk on honey
and I am drunk with spring sweetness
sip after sip

Water and Wine

The poets are gathering at the Piano Bar again —
the big and the small, the short and the tall —
they're all there
tuning their throats and scoffing water and wine.

There are the stutterers
and the mutterers
the ones with nifty threads
the singers and the wingers
but not a one with dreads.

There's a little bit of shuffling
to get them all in place
and a little bit of muttering
about the lack of space.

Progression is a problem
with people jumping in
and getting black looks from the rest
for such a dreadful sin.

I think we need a blackboard
to keep us all in line
but at least there are no fisticuffs
our manners turn out fine

in the end…

WALKING

Today, she walks with the sun[2]
while in her footsteps
the rain still falls

Today, she walks with the sun
and holds it inside her eyes
rising across the dark hills
where only the eagle flies

the sun moves on
leaving darkness where it has passed
until the morning

---

2   from 'Today she walks with the sun' by Hone Tuwhare in *Small Holes in the Silence: Collected Poems*.

AUSTIN KLEON[3]

Austin says
anger is a creative resource
but what happens
when things get so bad
that your anger closes its ears
and crawls into
a hole in the ground
to die?

---

3   *Steal like an artist: 10 things nobody told you about being creative* by Austin Kleon.

This Day

Red berries on the deck
among flashing swords
of nikau.

Sun-warmed wind
soft on my skin.

The shifting Paulownia leaves
painting shadow patterns
over the pebbles
with gentle hand claps.

Sound of birds.
A horse snorts
from the paddock.
Somewhere a dog barks.

In this sun, this wind, this day
I remember you.

Missing

My dear friend nowhere in sight[4]
and the train will leave at any moment
taking me away from this place
and these dreams.

I thought he might come
elbowing the curious crowd
maybe riding a white horse
just for me

but the train whistle blows
and I am gone.

---

4   from 'Mourning Meng Hao-Jan', by Wang Wei, in *Classical Chinese Poetry: An Anthology*, translated and edited by David Hinton.

Journey

in my heart we are still young
you and I, although the road narrows
and the river runs turbulent
to the sea
the dance is slower now
as winter fingers our bones
and finds them brittle

To the City

airport
electronic announcements
swallowed
in the silence

curve of a cloud front
over the Pacific
and the thin surf line
of the coast
where Taranaki
crouches brown
above the plains

below the motorway
a convocation of hard-hats
orange-vested men
measuring changes

city streets
moving to the music
of the dance
a homeless man
asking for change

hot city night
down on the pavement
guys are dealing
from the back of a car
small men swaggering
from the shadows
seeking dreams
or oblivion

LOVE

these things are true:
the curve of a petal
an autumn leaf, falling
iridescent flash of a kingfisher wing

sound of raindrops on dry earth
wind scything grass
sunlight on clouds
softness of a single snowflake

the journey of rivers to the sea
pebbles on a beach
moonlight on water
the calling home at evening

Memories

my old phone had a memory
with numbers saved
to ring my family

sometimes I would push the buttons
for my mother
even though I knew
that she was no longer there

just knowing her number
was still on my phone

then the phone got too old
as my mother had
and now I have a new phone
with no memories

If you have enjoyed Seen From the Gallery, please leave a review on the website of the seller you purchased it from. Good reviews are the life blood of independently-published authors, so please take a few moments to let others know what you thought of the book.

Thank you for reading.

www.wordlypress.com

www.ingramcontent.com/pod-product-compliance
Lightning Source LLC
LaVergne TN
LVHW010035070426
835507LV00006B/140